For Brian & Jo
– SGC

Sital Gorasia Chapman is passionate about bringing math to life for kids. She worked in finance before becoming a children's author.

Consultant Steph King works with elementary school educators to improve math teaching and learning in the classroom. She has written many math books for children.

 Penguin Random House

Author Sital Gorasia Chapman
Mathematics Advisor Steph King
Illustrator Susanna Rumiz

Editors Laura Gilbert, Rea Pikula
US Senior Editor Shannon Beatty
Senior Designer Rachael Parfitt Hunt
Production Editor Becky Fallowfield
Senior Production Controller Leanne Burke
Jacket Coordinator Elin Woosnam
Managing Editor Penny Smith
Managing Art Editor Anna Hall
Art Director Mabel Chan
Publisher Francesca Young

First American Edition, 2025
Published in the United States by DK Publishing, a division of Penguin Random House LLC
1745 Broadway, 20th Floor, New York, NY 10019

Text copyright © Sital Gorasia Chapman 2025
Artwork and design copyright © 2025 Dorling Kindersley Limited

25 26 27 28 29 10 9 8 7 6 5 4 3 2 1
001–342124–Jun/2025

All rights reserved.
Without limiting the rights under the copyright reserved above, no part of this publication may be reproduced, stored in or introduced into a retrieval system, or transmitted, in any form, or by any means (electronic, mechanical, photocopying, recording, or otherwise), without the prior written permission of the copyright owner.
Published in Great Britain by Dorling Kindersley Limited

A catalog record for this book is available from the Library of Congress.
ISBN: 978-0-5939-6537-5

DK books are available at special discounts when purchased in bulk for sales promotions, premiums, fund-raising, or educational use.
For details, contact: DK Publishing Special Markets, 1745 Broadway, 20th Floor, New York, NY 10019
SpecialSales@dk.com

Printed and bound in China

www.dk.com

This book was made with Forest Stewardship Council™ certified paper – one small step in DK's commitment to a sustainable future. For more information go to www.dk.com/our-green-pledge

The Math Adventurers

Make a Difference

DK

Beep and Boots wanted to borrow a book.
So they went to the library to have a good look.

They noticed the shelves
looked a little bit bare,

and they'd already read
all the books that were there.

"Let's buy them some more," Beep said with a smile.

They went to the bookstore and browsed through the aisles.

$5

2 for 1

Money comes in coins and bills. Each one has a different value. Smaller coins and bills can be added together to make a larger amount. Boots has a $1 bill and a 25¢ coin (called a quarter). They can be added together to make $1.25.

They filled up a cart and lined up to pay...

"We have to do something to raise some more cash to fill up the bookshelves..."

...and then in a flash—

Beep had an idea.
"Let's have a school fair!"
They met up with friends
and began to prepare.

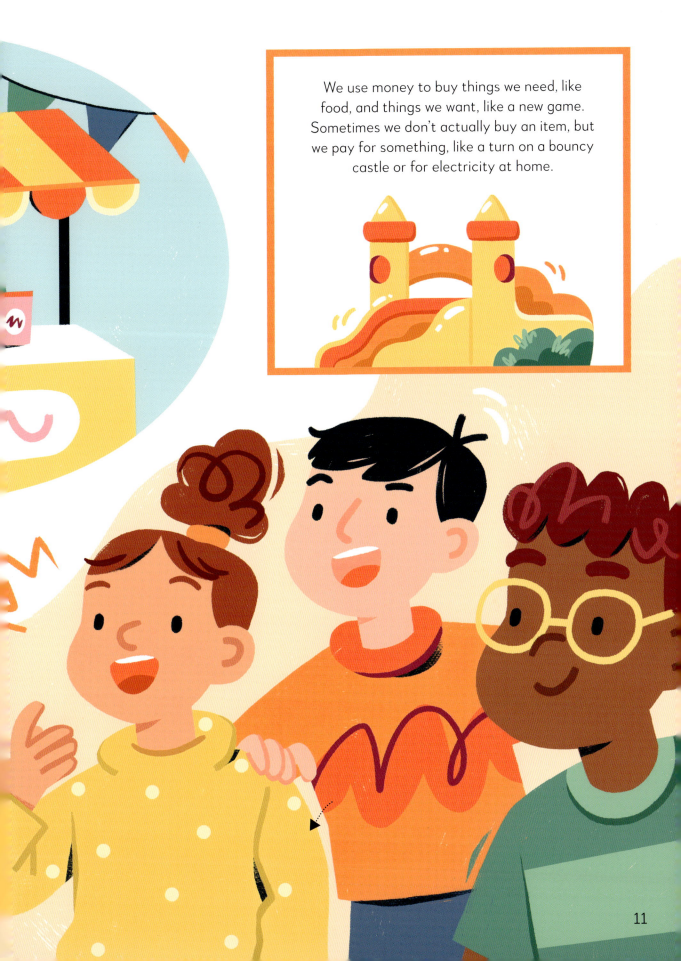

We use money to buy things we need, like food, and things we want, like a new game. Sometimes we don't actually buy an item, but we pay for something, like a turn on a bouncy castle or for electricity at home.

To make at least $300 was the plan, to buy 60 books. "If we try hard, we can!"

They collected donations
to sell on the day.
They figured out the prices
that people would pay.

They mapped out the stalls
and gathered supplies.
Then they put up some posters
to help advertise.

The big day arrived.
The weather was great.
And a crowd was waiting
at the school gate.

Popcorn $1

Juice 50¢ or
3 cups for $1

$1
$2
$3
$4

It is important to check that we have enough money to buy the items we want. One of the children has $4 to spend. Do they have enough to paint pottery and make two paper planes?

There were snacks and drinks and toys to buy.
There were arts and crafts, and a treasure hunt to try.

ARTS and CRAFTS

Make a paper plane
$1

Paint pottery
$2

Find the gold coins on the treasure hunt
$3

James spent $1.50 on popcorn and juice.

Lily paid $3 for a cuddly toy moose.

Roxy spent $2 to paint a piggy bank.

Anaya paid $1 for a bag full of blocks.

When we do not have the exact bills and coins to buy things, we give a larger amount of money and we get some change back. The change is the difference between the cost of the things we buy and the money we give.

The fair was bustling,
a huge success.
The children excited,
the teachers impressed.

PAY HERE

And the best stall of all, run by Boots and Beep, where big and little kids could jump and leap...

was the bouncy castle, fitting five at a time. Kids waited eagerly in a very long line.

Beep took the payments, charged $1 a turn.
Boots counted out change and the money they earned.

One of the children does not have exactly $1, so they pay with a $5 bill. How much change do they get?

They worked really hard.
The fair came to an end.
The people went home,
and Beep turned to her friend,

"Let's have a try.
I've been waiting all day!"
She paid for their turns
and they both bounced away.

The stalls were packed up.
It was time to find out
if they'd raised enough money.
They started to count.

$100 from the food and drinks sold.

$50 made from the search for the gold.

When we want to find a money total, we must add up all the amounts. The bouncy castle made $220. How much money did they raise in total? How much more than their $300 target was this?

$50 raised from the arts and crafts made.
And for the toys, in total, $80 paid.

To reach their target,
just $20 needed.
Had they done it?
Yes! They succeeded!

23

Beep and her friends were feeling so great! They went to the bookstore and filled up a crate

with tales of adventure and stories to scare, words of wonder and poems to share.

Books for learning and books just for fun. They carefully chose them one by one.

"We have 100 books!"
Beep squealed in delight.
But did they have enough money?

Yes, it's just right!

We can use what we know about counting with numbers to help us count with money? We can count 20 fives up to 100. How many $5 books can Beep and Boots buy for $100? How many $5 books can they buy for $500?

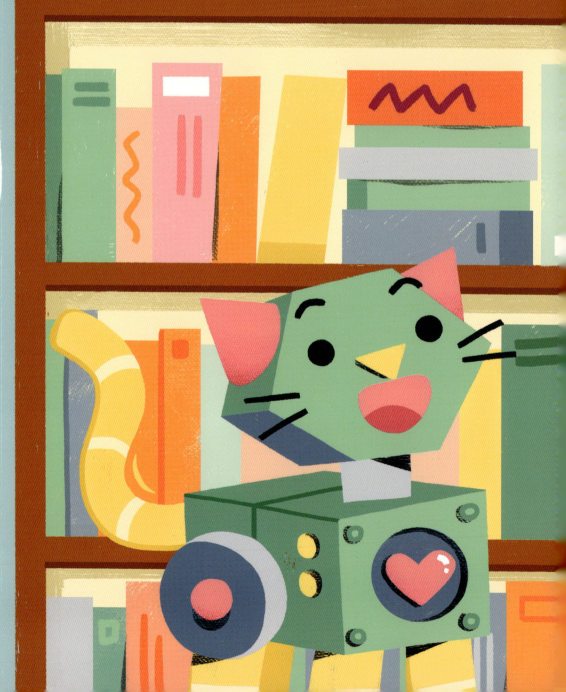

They stacked them all up
from ceiling to floor,
filled bookshelves to bursting.
Couldn't fit any more.

"There must be a way we can fit more books in...

Let's build a bigger library!" Beep said with a grin.

GLOSSARY

Pay—to give money in exchange for the things we buy

Coins—metal money

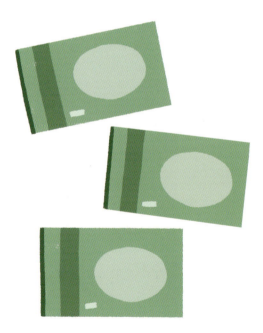

Bills—paper money

Currency—the type of money used in a country

Penny—a unit of currency

Dollar—a unit of currency. There are 100 pennies in a dollar

Change—the money left over when you pay for something with more money than it costs

Price—the amount of money something is offered on sale for

QUESTIONS

1. Beep buys a drink for 50¢ and popcorn for $1. How much does she spend in total?

2. One turn on the bouncy castle costs $1. One child pays for themselves and a friend with a $10 bill. How much change would they get?

3. Beep has 5 turns on the bouncy castle. How much does she spend?

4. Boots has three bills. How much money does she have in total?

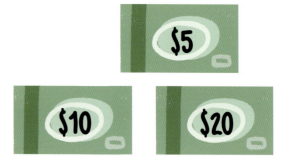

5. Beep has $3. A book costs $5. How much more does she need to buy a book?

6. Boots has $2.50. She wants to buy a gift for Beep. Which of these can she afford?

7. Which of these foods is the cheapest?

8. Which is the most expensive?

9. Beep has $7. She buys a banana every day for a week. How much does she have left?

10. If a book costs $5, how many can you buy for $50?

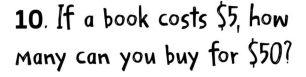

ANSWERS

1. $1.50
2. $8
3. $5
4. $35
5. $2
6. The pack of pencils or the sticky notes.
7. The banana
8. The grapes
9. Nothing!
10. 10

Fact box ANSWERS

p.14: Yes

p.19: $4

p.23: They raised $500. This is $200 more than their target of $300.

p.25: They can buy 20 books for $100. They can buy 100 books for $500.